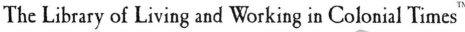

The Library of Living and Working in Colonial Times™

A Day in the Life of a Colonial Lighthouse Keeper

Laurie Krebs

The Rosen Publishing Group's
PowerKids Press™
New York

For my friend, Anne Gaston
With thanks to Christine Jones, Park Ranger, Boston Harbor Islands, National Park Area

Published in 2004 by The Rosen Publishing Group, Inc.
29 East 21st Street, New York, NY 10010

First Edition

Editor: Frances E. Ruffin
Book Design: Emily Muschinske

Photo Credits: Cover and title page (left), pp. 4, 7 (inset), 16 © Jeremy D'Entrement; cover (inset) and title page (right) © Hulton Archive; pp. 4 (inset), 15, 20 © United States Lighthouse Society; pp. 7, 11, 12, 19 © North Wind Pictures; p. 8 © The Mariners' Museum, Newport News, Virginia.

Krebs, Laurie.
A day in the life of a colonial lighthouse keeper / by Laurie Krebs.— 1st ed.
    p. cm. — (The library of living and working in colonial times)
Includes bibliographical references and index.
  ISBN 0-8239-6226-1
1. Boston Light (Mass.)—Juvenile literature. 2. Lighthouse keepers—Massachusetts—Juvenile literature.
I. Title. II. Series.
  VK1025.B6 K74 2003

                                                            2001005472

Thomas Knox was a real lighthouse keeper of the Boston Light. Mr. Knox's day-to-day responsibilities as they appear in this book are factual, but the details describing those responsibilities are fictional.

Manufactured in the United States of America

Contents

The Keeper at Boston Light

It was early evening as Thomas Knox climbed to the lighthouse lantern room. In 1783, colonial lighthouse keepers, such as Thomas, tended the huge oil lamps that guided sailing ships into port at night.

Boston Light, on Little Brewster Island, overlooked Boston Harbor. Thomas carried up whale oil to fuel the lamps. He wound a large clock that kept the lights inside the lamps turning. A shaft of light fell across the choppy water below. A storm was on the way.

◄ *This is a modern photograph of Boston Light.*
Inset: Boston Light has 76 steps to the top.

Boston Harbor

Thomas wanted to be a lighthouse keeper like his father and grandfather before him. As a boy, he watched sailors working on the ships. Thomas loved everything about the sea.

However, when fog blanketed the coastline and the sea stirred into angry foam, he knew the vessels were in danger. Along New England's rocky coast, many ships were tossed against the **shoals** and broken into pieces. Sometimes it was only the tower's beam that guided sailors safely to shore.

This 1775 map shows Boston Harbor, a busy colonial seaport. Inset: This is a modern-day picture of the lighthouse. ▶

Winifnit

Prospect Hill

Road to Cambridge
Charles Town Common

Pleasant Hill

Mill Dam

Phipps

Bunker Hill

CHARLES TOWN

CHARLES RIVER

Stores & Floating Battery

Ships & Floating Batteries

Noddles I

Mill Pond

North Battery

Bacon Hill

Bowdoin House

Common

Hancock's Warf

BOSTON TOWN

HARBOUR

Long Warf

South Battery

I Parl

Fortification

Flat

Boston Neck

Roxbury Hill

Thomas's Camp & Lines

Road to Roxbury

Road to Dorchester

Governors I

BOSTON AND VICINITY, JUNE, 1775.

To the Merchants of Boston this View of the LIGHT HOUSE *is most humbly presented By their Humble Serv.t W.m Burgis*

Under British Rule

Thomas remembered the year 1775, when Boston and the lighthouse had been controlled by the British. They blocked the harbor so only British ships could enter.

As the **American Revolution** drew closer, the colonists set fire to Boston Light so the British could not use it. The British repaired the damage. In June 1776, as the British left Boston, they destroyed the lighthouse again.

After America gained **independence**, the lighthouse was rebuilt on the same spot. Thomas became its keeper in 1783.

◀ *The new lighthouse was built with stones from the original one. Here a British ship sails in front of Boston Light.*

Lighthouses of Long Ago

Lighthouses were not new in Thomas's day. The first lighthouse was built in Alexandria, Egypt, around 280 B.C. It was called Pharos and stood 450 feet (137 m) tall! Priests tended a fire at the top of the tower to signal to the sailors below.

Boston Light, built in 1716, was the first lighthouse in colonial America. By the time of the American Revolution 60 years later, eleven more lighthouses lined the East Coast. Most were built along New England's rocky coast.

The lighthouse in Alexandria, Egypt, guided ▶
ships to safety.

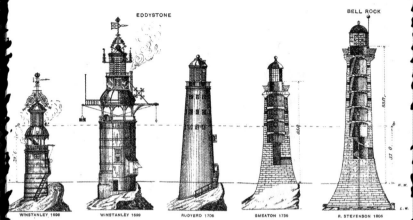

EDDYSTONE

BELL ROCK

WINSTANLEY 1696

WINSTANLEY 1699

RUDYERD 1706

SMEATON 1756

R. STEVENSON 1808

a, b. HEIGHT AT WHICH 14 JOGGLED STONES, SET IN PORTLAND CEMENT, WERE SWEPT OFF AT DHUHEARTACH

SCALE

0   5   10   20   30   40   50   60   70   80   90   100 Feet.

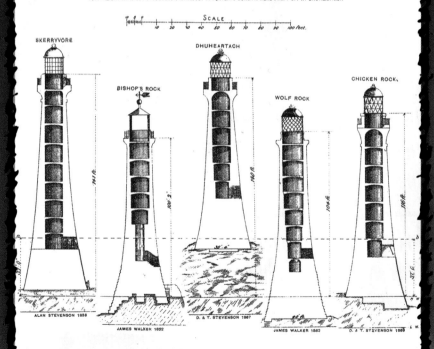

SKERRYVORE

DHUHEARTACH

CHICKEN ROCK

BISHOP'S ROCK

WOLF ROCK

ALAN STEVENSON 1838

D. & T. STEVENSON 1867

JAMES WALKER 1852

JAMES WALKER 1862

D. & T. STEVENSON 1869

Lighthouse Design

Early American lighthouses were made from wood, stone, or brick. Thomas Knox's Boston Light was white and pointed at the top.

If lighthouses were built on flat land, they were built tall so that they could be seen. If they stood on high cliffs, they were built low and wide. Their colors differed, too. Some lighthouses were red or black. Some had stripes painted on them. The differences in the colors and the patterns of lighthouses were called daymarks. They made it easy for a ship's captain to tell where he was.

◀ *Different lighthouses were designed for different shoreline conditions.*

A Busy Night

Thomas kept an eye on the changing weather. The wind picked up and sheets of rain rattled the windows. Heavy fog hid the coastline. Thomas couldn't see a thing from the tower. He climbed down to the cannon kept at the bottom of the light.

He fired the cannon across the water. A ship close to the shore heard the warning. The ship sounded its cannon in reply just in time! Then Thomas ran up the tower to tend the flame. He ran down again to fire the cannon every hour until the storm ended.

This window in the Boston Light lighthouse faces ▶
Boston Harbor.

A Job Well Done

When things were quiet again, Thomas had regular tasks to manage. It was Thomas's job to light the lamps at sunset, keep them burning all night, and **snuff** them out at sunrise. He also kept the cannon ready to signal on foggy days. He polished brass **fixtures** and made small repairs to the building. He painted the lighthouse inside and out. He kept a daily **log** of the weather and an account of the whale oil he used. That wasn't all. At times he had to climb outside the tower to fix it. That was a very dangerous job.

◀ *This is the cannon that once sat at the base of the Boston Light lighthouse.*

To the Rescue

Thomas also had to rescue sailors. Once, a raging storm made the sky terribly dark. It was hard to tell day from night.

A **schooner** ran into the rocks just off the coast of Little Brewster Island. Sailors were thrown into the sea. Their lifeboats broke up on the rocky shoals. Thomas jumped into his boat and rowed out to save the men. The waves were 10 feet (3 m) high! He reached the men just in time, but both the schooner and its contents were lost. Thomas knew the men were lucky to reach the shore safely.

Ships at sea during rough storms often were in danger. ▶

A Keeper's Pay

To pay for the **upkeep** of the lighthouse, shipowners paid a fee when they entered or left the harbor. For local **trade** and fishing vessels, the price was five **shillings** per year.

The fee also paid Thomas's salary of $225 per year as head lighthouse keeper. He and his family were given a house on the island and 25 stacks of wood to keep it warm. There was good soil for a garden and plenty of fish to eat. Thomas was also given the use of a boat to earn extra money as a harbor pilot. He guided ships safely into port.

◀ *A house for the lighthouse keeper was part of the keeper's pay.*

Life on Brewster Island

The sky had cleared as Thomas Knox put away his polishing cloths and climbed down the 2 ladders and 76 steps. It was time for a warm breakfast and a chat with his wife.

The Knox family lived on Little Brewster Island year-round. In good weather, they gardened and enjoyed picnics.

Thomas waved to his children. They were leaving on a small boat for school on the **mainland**. Thomas smiled as he looked out at the calm ocean and thought, yes, there will be safe passage for sailors tonight.

Glossary

American Revolution (uh-MER-uh-ken reh-vuh-LOO-shun) Battles that soldiers from the American colonies fought against England for freedom from 1775 to 1783.

fixtures (FIHKS-cherz) Things added as part of a ship or building.

independence (in-dih-PEN-dents) Freedom from the control, support, or help of other people.

log (LAHG) A record, usually written, of day-to-day activities.

mainland (MAYN-land) A large area of land near an island.

schooner (SKOO-ner) A two-masted, rigged ship.

shillings (SHIH-lingz) Coins formerly used in Great Britain and the colonies.

shoals (SHOHLZ) Sandbars that make the water shallow.

snuff (SNUHF) To put out a candle or other flame.

trade (TRAYD) The business of buying and selling.

upkeep (UP-keep) The act of keepng things in good condition.

Index

Primary Sources

Page 7. *Map of Boston and Vicinity, June 1775.* This map is based on John Almon's map of Boston created in June 1775 and published in *The Remembrancer.* The original is held in the collections of the Library of Congress.

Page 8. *The Boston Light House.* This mezzotint by William Burgis was presented to the merchants of Boston. William Burgis was an engraver of maps and views between 1717 and 1731. This engraving of Boston Light is the only piece by Burgis on which his name appears. This copy is in the collection of the Mariners' Museum in Newport News, Virginia.

Page 19. This 1800s woodcut from North Wind Pictures shows a sailing ship in stormy seas. During colonial times sea voyages were often long and uncomfortable, and storms could be life-threatening. **Page 20.** This is an aquatint of the original Boston lighthouse from *The Keeper's Log,* the quarterly journal of the United States Lighthouse Society.

Web Sites

Due to the changing nature of Internet links, PowerKids Press has developed an online list of Web sites related to the subject of this book. This site is updated regularly. Please use this link to access the list:
www.powerkidslinks.com/llwct/dlclitk/